ONE

HOUR

MORE

DEREK MORLEY

Published by Sanderson

Sanderson Books

ISBN: 978-1-9994181-9-9

TABLE OF CONTENTS

DEDICATION

For Allyson

Rarely in life do we encounter a person who, for whatever reason is extremely compelling. Almost to the point of compulsion. A feeling of magical urgency. I think it is a blessing that its rare. While it's an incredible experience to be out of control and in love, in my case it was not an easy thing. It required of me much overcoming. Allyson was a powerful teacher to not take things personally. To stand and contend with feelings of rejection. All such challenges were supportable because you're bright and beautiful and beloved. You roused in me an imperative to grow. I make this book to convey my gratitude for the impact you've had on my life, just by being you. A solid artifact imbued with my love for you. I hope beyond hope that it serves you as well as it has served me.

ACKNOWLEDGMENT

I'm convinced that the meaning of life is measured and meted out in relationship. So first up I'd like to acknowledge the loving support of my community of friends who steadied me through the rough moments and thus helped make this book possible. Special thanks go to Kate C., Julie G. and Yafa G. who provided me with feedback and reflections with particular care for my he(art). Thank you to my publisher and long-time friend, Crystal Elizabeth Westman, who encouraged me to continue with the intention to publish with Sanderson. Thanks to Glenn Evans for the cover. Thanks to the innumerable authors who have inspired me and cultivated my love of letters; Marshall Mcluhan, Rumi, Tom Robbins, Doestoevsky, Ursula K. Leguin.

INTRODUCTION

The writing of this book began as a reflexive attempt to cope with an experience that I had never had before; a rejection that was a sudden break which seemed to be absolutely final. What made it still more peculiar is that my partner communicated this choice as an instruction received in a vision from God. In the context of her church and belief system, such visions were not particularly unusual or astonishing, but from my perspective I had no idea how to integrate it or make sense of it. Fair to say it threw me for a loop

I have had my own complex relationship with Christianity to contend with. My father ostensibly belonged to the Anglican church but found his sacrament in LSD. My mother was a Catholic almost as a by-product of being French Canadian. They got around to baptizing me when I was 8 years old, at the request of the school. Neither of them had much interest in a relationship with the church and I don't recall ever entering a church with my father. Nevertheless, they directed my education to Catholic schools. There I faithfully carried the imprint of my father's cynicism of religion. He loved to talk about the big topics and in his discourses and reflections on the meaning of life, which he would often share with me or anyone who would listen, there was a shadow of a god-fearing upbringing. He would never admit to it, but it could occasionally be felt as a subtle undercurrent. He was a bon-vivant and although his reading was limited, he pieced together a charming world view from the likes Tolkien, Hesse, Gilbran, Castenada.

Inheriting my father's explicit and my mother's more implicit counter culture rebellion, I felt out of place in Catholic school. It was a case of not finding an inroad to the magic of the sacrament. We didn't believe as they believed. I was also primed to be critically disposed towards any authority figures.

In my view, the teachers all fell short of the lofty ideals that were communicated in the moral instruction of the church. Of course, they did, as we all must. At the time, I could only interpret that as hypocrisy. I was terribly naive about it all and only felt the sense of not belonging.

In the intervening decades, I have witnessed so many subtle shades of the sacred; from Brazil to Bangkok, India and looking inward. I met a Mexican pastor who restored my faith in Christianity, and I have seen mass graves unearthed that questioned my faith in humanity. I had come to terms with religion and with spirituality - so I had thought. But whatever sense of contentment and equanimity I had was shaken by this experience.

A combination of the strong shock of her sudden disappearance coupled with the impression of a religious judgment against me personally activated unresolved traumas from my youth. I was so disoriented by the impact of this double effect that I didn't immediately realize what was happening. By the grace of God or goodness or what have you, I found the poetic enterprise. The creation of this book then emerges as a synthesis of two distinct and parallel purposes- or let's say, needs of mine- at the time.

The first was to provide a locus to map out the emotional terrain I was experiencing. That is, to draw out the venom of the break-up and the hidden pain arising from and through the harmonic resonance between this present event and the painful dissonance of my earlier estrangement with religion.

The second purpose was to give me a space to communicate with her, because I always assumed I would one day deliver to her a copy of the book.

In the interim, I was sharing some of the poems online and I knew she was reading them, we even had some brief exchanges about them from time to time. I fully believed in her good intention towards me then, and still to this day. I thought that she may have been unaware of the effects and consequences of her choices and I wanted to share with her an uncensored view of them. It is a central idea of mine that "Legitimate suffering has the power to purify and make wise." That only works when we are honest and open about it.

In sharing the work online with my community, the commiseration which I received was a blessing. Occasionally I would get a message from someone of how a poem had helped them access and confront a grieving or loss of their own. These little graces added up and emerged as a concurrent motivation for the writing. Poets are particularly vulnerable to the insidious idea that our craft is not essential. These small encouragements shored up my resolve to grant myself the time necessary to see it through to completion. A vision emerged of a book that could give a real-time reporting of a heart's ambition to understand the beloved with full compassion and to validate her experience while honoring my own, through a total breakdown. The result is a collection of poems that show an irregular oscillation in disposition. A quasi-schizophrenic dance that strives to reach a resolution. The vicissitudes of trust and doubt, self-awareness and naivete, are among the essential themes.

In our modern times, music is so often the "soundtrack" of our lives. Art influences life and life reciprocates. I sometimes wonder what life would be like if we didn't have access to such an unfathomably large catalogue of incredibly powerful and intricate music. How do we survive the casual access to all the potency of it all? In this story music was constantly present. We got to know each other through shared playlists. The influence of music is an essential part of this book, and so I've created a playlist to accompany the reading of it, one song per poem. I suggest a reading of the book accompanied by the playlist, dwelling on each poem for the duration of the song before moving onto the next.

Incidentally, I did get the chance to deliver the book to her in person, as I had imagined. It was a private reading. The outcome was a lot of crying on both parts and hugs. Then, in the following weeks, a series of conversations and a reconciliation. It was to be short-lived. We dated again for about 6 weeks. Owing to our fundamental incompatibilities, we ended up very much as we did the first time.

All of the poems in this volume are written between January 17th and May 5th. Only one poem was added to this edition after that time. It serves as the epilogue to this little booklet.

MELTING

From the very first flirtations
Consecrated conversations
Over Stave and Steel
At the empty house
Of the traveling Brazilians

From first touch and first temptation
Billions of milli-seconds
        Congregating to sanction
            An imminence
                That wanted to be.

From the first
We had to contend with
            Tremendous potential

We were sped on angel's wings
On the canvas of our bodies,
Emotions expressed

The joy of being a lover
Who seeks to know the self
Through lovers' eyes.

And the obstacles...
                How to proceed?

So, we set to laying foundations

Making well-considered lists
Of all we wanted in a mate

                    Bless our hearts
And non-negotiables we
Couldn't do without
Though we
Really
Couldn't comprehend them

The biggest difference
Was plurality v monogamy
That's where I began
To feel you melt my heart

                    My tender heart

Had built an elaborate edifice of instructions
For how no one need hurt no more
An analysis of monogamy
That found it to be flawed
                              Skewed
In the foolish way
It asks us to group up in twos
Silo ourselves in containers
That inhibit the natural effusiveness of love

Relational structures that are
Necessarily fragile

For if one partner can go off the rails...
In a pair-bond, this is utterly destabilizing
Like an island with one bridge that fails

But in a polyamorous web of connections
With many partners,
                    Some emotional,
                            Some spiritual,
                                    Some sexual,

When one person moves to   Malaysia
When someone goes away...
It doesn't have the destabilizing effect
That happens when a pair bond cracks in half

The web of connections holds us up
                            Antifragile

This intricate construction,
Sophistry,
Extended into conviction,
I decorated
        And lived in,
        For decades.
        Developed, and
        There made a happy home.

It simply seemed
We dreamed different dreams

But

The intensity of your devotion
The sheer joy of your nearness
Awoke memories in me and desires
That had not been spoken...

For so long
They'd almost been forgotten
                    Laying dormant
                    The bedrock of my soul

That bedrock upon which all
Cathedrals had been built
Heated up by the heat between us
Grew red hot and I watched,

Astonished
All of my well reasoned arguments
                                    Wilted

Desire from within me
To be in deep partnership intensified
Teetering towers dripped and melted

Like a great beeswax candle
On a hotplate
                Suddenly
                        It was too late

I was undone

Discovering myself
In love with you

As every aspect of life was redefined
And everything became itself with Ally

And
   time
      itself
        became
          like
            h
             o
              n
               e
              y

SAYONARA

Her words landed like a sentence
That a guilty man fears
Is clairvoyance creation?
Do we author with our dreams?

On the frigid night of January 17th
She put a swift end to our relations
Visions put to extremes
Something I seemed to see coming

Vision from God
That we were not meant to be together
T'would be better not to waste precious time
Our two paths already diverging
Two glorious and separate futures
I'll be happier with a different girl

What's this?
But...
Isn't there something I can do or say?

Something to adjust?

To make better for you?

Did I break your trust?

Did I hurt your heart?

Is there something to mend?

"No"

She simply said.

"You don't understand,
Everything was perfect
No complaints to speak of
This is the biggest sacrifice
ever asked of me"

In that decision
She gave me no say
It was fait accompli
Unilaterally

"I love you, goodbye."

Make that make sense for me.

CHURCH ONE

Or….
                was it something I uttered,
While I was poorly,
With COVID, on the mend?
Surely you can comprehend…
I think I was hit in an old wound then

Triggered

When you said, "saved"
It sounded like slander.

Just as a coin has two sides wedded,
Saved implies unsaved does it not?

Arrogance embedded
In the language engraved
Incidentally damning
All bystanders.

This implication meanders
From your intent, I am sure
But in no uncertain prose
The church that talks about "saved"
Insists that God only wear THEIR clothes

But does this critique cleave

A divide between us?
Make impure the holy waters?

Your strategic retreat is cloaked
With mysteries and questions dangling.
Visions from God?
A divine commandment?

    That seems a little odd.

       You have either a god complex

   Or a complex god.

The paragon Christ I do adore

I think it's enough
To do more to uphold
The Christlike path
And profess less

It's not a questions of the bath
It's a test of how we live and love each day

 Alas
     Too late
         You're gone
             Nothing
                To say

SABOTEUR

An illative reader of souls might never have
spoken
Words so ill-conceived
Almost devised to self-destruct
To haunt the fractured corners of the mind

Search as I may I cannot find
Any reason why
I let my tongue fly
And denigrate all that she loves

Intellectual flotsam and jetsam
Calamity to my cherished hope
I rent a hole in my own boat
Spouting loquacious instead of
The true feeling of my heart

Days that feel like weeks and months unfold
A scramble for land to stand upon
For meaning in the maelstrom
And all the intervening states
Full of what I feel and feel and feel

An intuitive and faithful man

Could perhaps do a better job than I
Such as I am I cannot fly
Beyond a common bound
And common blunders
I can't help wonder what might have been?

I know any cynic can certainly
Compete concurrent with the Worst
To devise devious, doubtful descriptions
For every miracle,
That happens here on earth.

Temptation to dwell among the doubters
Hurts

No

One

More

Than

Ourselves

So I try to hitch my heart to a flying star
And focus on the blessing of my breath
And disregard the matter of her breast
And make the most of blessed days
Of which we have
So few upon the earth

If I had never spoken it in the first
May I be allowed to
Believe it might be worse?

That we would hold each other back and so
That if I love her, I must really let her go

Oh I would love to believe in that

But from where I'm standing now
It's landing
Flat.

DESTINY

The sudden incomprehensible loss of you
Fills me with grief at
                              The rapid
               Reversal

Utterly loved in reciprocity
You were my person
Until   Maddeningly   Not

Weren't we locked in 9-0
And taking it seriously?

Love came alive between us
I felt the resonance and encouragement
I wonder where it went?
Or who discouraged it?
I struggle to believe God frowns on our love
Did the other man make you doubt your
worthiness?

     Speak truth,

               Please!

               Why are you doing this?

You had a vision that we wouldn't work?
Or you just can't reconcile the strands of
your life?

I'm disoriented in this story,
At some moment I lost the plot
I can only grasp at the threads

I know where you are
But I cannot
Reach you

"I want you to have the best life you can
have"

That phrase passed your lips

Do you think you have a better life waiting?

Or that I do?
                              Or both

And yet, what could be better than what we
were sharing?

SHOTS FIRED

The morning after you discharged me
I held awareness of our bond
Like a sculpture in my hand.
Ever so slowly, while I made coffee
In that beautifully bright kitchen
I watched it phase shift
From solid into sand

I was immediately transferred
To emotional field medic duty
So I took myself for a walk on the frozen land
Gasping crisp cool January air
I wandered through the deep snow trails
Feeling the steadying still of the spruce
forest
Lighting a fire in the wood stove

I think I was trying to "take it like a man"
How ever is a man to take a shot to the
heart?

"Just do the best you can, it's never easy
But it will pass" I could hear the voices
bolstering
Even as the gun was holstering
Without the slightest argument or heat

Without any disagreement of which to speak
I'd been replaced
Who was beloved
From David to a skeet

ON THE JOB

Don't take life too seriously,
God is on the job
But take care of yourself
It's my wish for you

Don't miss your chance
To make the world a better place
With a simple smile
Or a thoughtful word

If you're quiet in mind
Not whining about what's past
You can hear a voice
Revealing your path

She wants you to shine
To expand in faith
Your doubts are all misplaced
What good do they do?

God is on the job
The signs of his divine hand
Are everywhere apparent
And she wants you to shine

Recollect the texture
Of your time together
The signs were all along the road
This is meant to make you better

Blame not yourself
It's not the failure you imagine
Prepare your conviction
For your glorious future

"Stop carrying me around"
She wishes in sincerity
Stop suffering and move on
Start to gather clarity

Your time is not to be wasted
You deserve the biggest yes
Your authentic self smile
I encourage, be blessed

When you arrive to your home
You will be greeted
With maximum love
And every encouragement

Did you forget for a second
That god has a plan
We understand as best we can
Most high fidelity

    You'll live on in my heart
    In ways you can't understand
    Today that's what matters
    I want you to shine

THERE WILL BE BETTER DAYS

A growing awareness and acceptance of
fragility

> Is now a part of me
> It's showing up as
> Tears in the chamber
> Locked and loaded.

My mind is not the same one I had before

And I'm sure that the   coin
Is still in the air
We are spin paired, high-energy, outcome
unknown

Could I become that person prophesied
In an active vision of capability
A wink at who I might or never be
High-functioning me- my destiny- or just
ADHD?

As I chose among the mugs for which to use
Making lemon ginger tea
I pick the tall one from the Costa Rica airport
Because   You gave it to me
I winced when I saw it sitting there
Then grabbed it masochistically

Gathering groceries with the usual care
To save a dollar here and there
Your memory
                    Mugs me
                              In the wine isle

Robbed of self-possession, I remember
Sauvignon pairs so well with your smile

Perhaps you aspire to tracelessness
I'm the determined detective who can't
Catch a clue
What's imagined and what's true

You're reckless!

And yes, me too

Do I need to vilify you??

Isn't there a story where no one is to blame?
Why does my pain bend to defame you?
Why can't I let you go from my life of your
own accord?
Instead, I tantrum, pout and call you names
Mostly bound inside my swollen head.

If you had loved me less, I'd be better off
You touched me too much for then to just

Stop

Less would have been more

    Too sharp

                The contrast

The cliff

Too hard the floor

At first, I was so thirsty for the high of
redemption

Visions of you taking me back, tears in eyes.
Wouldn't that be nice?

I tried

I'd have drunk the blood of Christ
And even liked it.

But you barred the door

You grabbed the chalice from my hand.
You say I'm blameless

You consume

Command

And crash it to the floor
No friendly drop for me

No more

CHURCH TWO

Oh, I how I love to wrestle with thee
Like Jacob in the night
You test my strength
And I want to get it right

Church is the body of Christ,
Where all the action happens
Church is revelation systematized
And heavy armor

I want to be in the church
That loves and uplifts its people
For me, church is much more
In the kitchen
Than in the steeple

Tomorrow I will go to church
To practice loving through failure
I'll be beautiful and sweet
Like Jesus in the manger

Tomorrow when I meet your church
I'll meet them with a conscience
That considers the consequence
Of my life, and all my actions

I'll come with open heart to church
To listen and to witness
I'll tell my heart to try it all
And fully go the distance

Then tomorrow if we meet at church
And I'm struck by emotion
I'll pray to God to steer me right
And honor every moment

I'll smile at everyone I see
And meet them all as family
The one who was so briefly mine
With such grace as I can find

RECHENSCHAFTSPFLICHT

I've given you so much of my love and
Trust that you didn't prove worthy of cause
There was never permitted any clause that
You abruptly cut ties and blame a God who

Needed you to drop me on a dime. It
Does not compute; a God who wanted
You to do that thing you chose to do. You
Fuck with the deepest feelings when you

Invoke religion to sterilize the choice and
Wipe your hands. You have free will, its
True. To own the choices you make, that's
All you have to do to
                    Be a responsible and mature adult

REVERENCE

How to be so rude to one who
Moves through life in ways
That are mysterious to you.
She somehow seems cruel or untrue
All to preserve you,

                       In your best interest.

How to say to someone who
Pushes you out of the way of oncoming
traffic

          "You pushed me! You bitch!"

It's tragic,

          These myopic things we do

Jettisoned

               Is how it seemed to you
How could she say

               "I love you"
And mean it
While tossing you off like an encumbrance
An evil seeming act,

A shrug

I struggle to grasp
The grace that redeems it

What do you need to see to believe it?
You said you trusted her with your whole
Heart

Patience please
The show has just begun
Take your seats
The action's not over
The drama not yet done

Did you want to live a life of perfect
simplicity?

Did you want to opt out of the mystery?

One that does not have gratitude

For the blessings life bestows

Dies miserably

FRAGILE

At my lowest point
Jealous and broken
Totally adrift
I drove by your house and noticed
His car in your lane

I went back to bed to refocus
But sleep wouldn't come
So I reread every passage and poem
Every message to unearth the truth

She had really loved me,

Hadn't she?

Or had I gone insane?

All night long I attended
To our story and felt reassured
That what we had shared was real

Bittersweet, to relive the whole ordeal

Tense and wired
Impatient in the icy morn
I hauled body and heart
Shamefaced to your door
But I didn't knock,
I called from the corner,
She answered the phone
"You can't come in, he's here"

OK

It's clear

Goodbye it is
"You deserve each other"
I stalked off in the frost

But I found courage to call you back that
night
Full of grief and tears and loss
I had to talk…
And you listened!
For two full hours
I filled your ears with rain
You held me through the worst of it

I think that's as close as I ever came
To seeing the world through your eyes

Or feeling your pain;
When you held me in mine

You did as best you could for me
Nothing either of us planned
Each one can only understand
To the level of comprehension they have

We can only see what we've seen

Only love as the love we've been given,
What we've been able to glean
Along the way

Such moments last forever
And can't be undone
Unexpected cruelty and kindness
Blended into one

AFASTADA

Foremost in the shape of grief
Rivers
    Of
       Pain,
          Tributaries
            That Flow
                To an ocean of sorrow

Is knowing it hurts you
            To see me suffer.
It doesn't in any solitary way
Make it even a sliver better

No

It wounds me to see my pain hurt you too

    Like the ocean reflecting
      The gun metal sky

Hall of mirrors madness
It all bleeds into the selfsame sadness

How could He not approve
Of a love like ours?
We shook numbness from the hearts
Of sweet and innocent fools
 Whenever the curtains part,

                                    I see you.

You cry, overwrought,
You ache, but stay the course.
I would commend you,
But it's the worst possible choice
Or so says that wounded little voice inside
my head

                    You're just gone,
                    And of course, the
                    choice is yours

I know you're suffering too
I see that clearly when you let me

There's no portion of calm
That I can give you
And that's just one more thing
                    That wrecks me

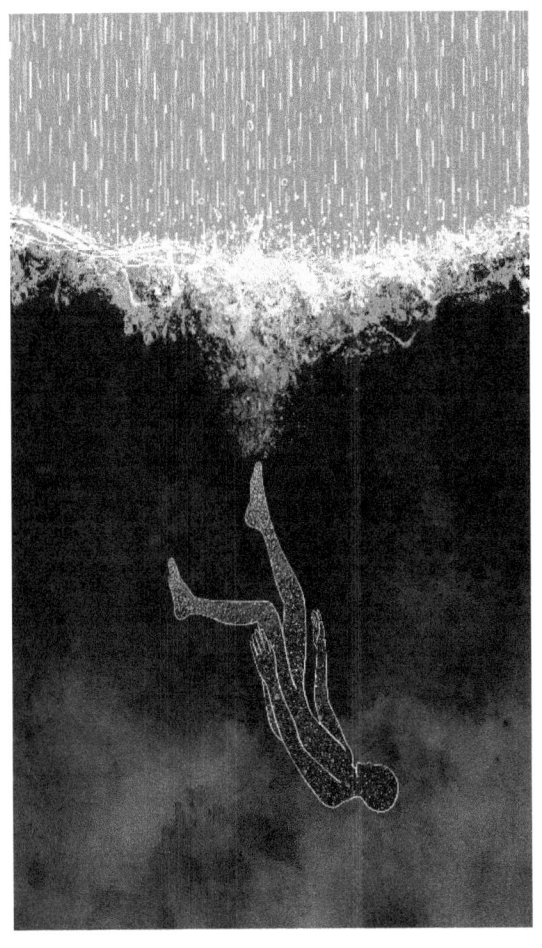

NON ACCEPTANCE

Cold

Stonewall of non-acceptance

And I am like a monkey trapped

        Fist inside the jar
        Stuck clinging

To what I cannot have

It's only as hard
As it is

Until I give up hope.

Let go.
        Release.

Every drop of blood I shed
Wandering among thorns
Is self-inflicted

        The dream is dead;
        It arrived still-born.

SO WE WON'T FORGET

How can we love ourselves?
How can we remember who we are?

As We are
All-in-one

Notice how often we select
Some to love
Some cast aside

Then we deign to decide
With scalpel mind
What to include and exclude
Incise and excise
Even sculpt our minds
And exercise our rights
To perform exorcism
On the aspects of self we don't like

Isn't it a schism craft
Exiling ugly aspects of ourselves
Uncelebrated and unloved
With mask and glove
Unceremoniously disregard
And determine to look upon no more

I don't believe it
Impossible to suppress
It's never lost
It remains embossed
Registered in some remote
Aspect of the self

Any elevated observer mind could tell
That it's all pretend
                    And pretense.
We can no more clip
                    Or prune any portion

Of our essential self
Than we can know where we will be
Tomorrow
                    And moreover

Why would we want to?
Subtract some so-called shameful selflet

We can be greater
And more authentic
More dynamic
In our filthy totality
As we remember that we are
All-in-one

                    The art of integration
                    Awaits the acolyte

SNEAKY

I can see I'm offloading my process
Into poetry
I want to be
But I don't get to be
Done because I make poems pretty

"So special"

Say my sarcastic angels

"Good job son, you get a biscuit
You turned it into words and missed it
You used all your might and strength

To keep the damned
thing at arm's length

No, you don't get to be done
Just because you're having fun
With words, you turd
You don't get to hyper-focus out
Don't be absurd
This art is not a tool to dodge this;
Time to dislodge it

This hijacking is really here
For you
To reckon with
Til it's digested
And the lessons torn
To the very core

Your process to explore
Goes deeper than expected
Truth deflected, does not disappear

To be sure
The choice is yours
The consequences too
Compounded by the passing years

Your path to walk,
Your process to clear
To honor as you can
And clip as you must"

I trust my angels are not wrong
I won't lose the forest for the trees

The book will be a tool for sure
And a damned poor substitute for her

BLACK MIRROR

The idea was fully formed
To fuck her
For a couple weeks at least.
Something simple, satisfying.
A delicious treat
I wanted to savor her
Like a beast
But that was before we'd really met
I was curious, but I wasn't attached
I just wanted to get my back scratched

I was intent on her, but patient, intrigued
Seize the day
Her salmon
Her table
I liked the way she trembled.
Wild, vulnerable, and I couldn't get enough

But she was not so good at naming and
Claiming what she wanted.
I wanted to play and
I was conquering her and
She was conquering me
With poetry

I could never imagine
What we would invoke
As we got closer and the pattern broke
Swept up in the scope of exhilarating sport

We flew

                But she was tethered and it tore

And we were thrown apart
As once before.

A sadistic joke
Celebrating recklessness as strength.

A curse on those who disturb
Civil peace with violent need.

If you let the baser urges rule you
They'll destroy your cherished hopes.

FORCE

If I had me a lasso
To rope the moon
I'd tie it to a lamppost to prolong the night
But I have no lid to tamp down the rising sun
The hope is in vain
Time keeps its own

Rhythm

There is no force I can bring
To bear on this love
That I can resolve it sooner

Or maybe ever

I can't love her better
I do not know how

The die is cast
No sweat of my brow
No, it's beyond my grasp

My wisdom
No matter
My money
No purchase
My charm
No bearing
My intuition
No clarity

I do not get to solve this.

I do not get to finesse this.

I do not get to "be in control."

I am utterly
                    At the mercy of time.

I feel like a kite taken by wind
All my confident capability

                    Is lost to me

                Leaving me feeling shaky.

The desire
To be secure,
            With no possibility of security

        Is the tornado that transports me

                Only
            In the stone heart of
                Acceptance

                I find calm
                And still

DAD

Hard to believe it's been
Near 5 years
Since you left the body
5 years   Goddam!
Thats a lot of time to spend
Don't ask me how much I'd love to hear your
voice again

Can I hear your heavenly council?
What on earth would you say
To this mess?

Some people have visions that guide
I have none
Even for those who have some,
The veils are layered thick
Maybe we're not meant to know.
I don't envy those who gets them
To tussle with destiny
Don't seem like too much fun

Your picture fell off the wall tonight, Dad
Of the many
It was the only one
That your way of just saying hello then, Dad?

"Wake up my boy!"

Sometimes I wonder if you're with me,
By my side
Of course you are!
But it doesn't stop the ache
That I can't hear your goddam stories no
more

      Or ask you why
          The fuck
             This thing
                Is happening to me?

But what could you say?
      I wish I could be sure.

Would you give me a big thumbs up?
Did I drop the ball?
Did we leave anything undone?

He speaks:
"Love is like a solar powered light that needs
the sun.
My son, my moon
The sun is gone just for a spell
Be strong, son
The sun sets for good reason
Only to rise again soon."

ONLY YOU

She may pretend not
But I know now,
She's afraid to see me
This thing that God asked her to do
Wasn't easy

She may be naive to the ways to proceed
But who wouldn't be?
Nobody prepared us
Not bible lessons nor history

For me it's tough,
I want to see her.
To see her would be a balm to pain.
     Remedy to loss,
         Even for just one minute
             Of infinite relief.

But even as I dissolve into grief and poetry
           She can't

She has to find the resolve to see it through
Painstakingly, for
it's   God's will

And she knows it

Is it any wonder she
Innocently avoids me.

We're both in this
But can't be in it together

Oh brawling love
        Convoluted torture

United in fervor
I know what it's cost me
To be without you.

But where will you be
When your time comes to pay?

And who will hold you
At the end of that day?

I'm afraid it can't

        While I

                Still
        Wish
                        It could
                        Be me

LIVING PRESENCE

I love my life,
By which I mean:
A collection of somatic wonders
That frequently form a tingling sensation
Around the borders of my body
Vibrating with joy and awe
That such raw phenomena exists at all

To have access to all this!
Born in this time and place,
Among vast scope
Of possible times and spaces;
This richness of culture and technology

To have and holf access to myself,
Through leisure and duty,
In balance and community.
Autonomy and ownership
Of who I am, and what I can make of my days

Blissful states of being
That cannot be continual
                              Normalized.

I authorize my life, to casually contain
The most exhilarating states of happiness

I belong to happiness as it belongs to me
Reasons and rich material abundant daily
To mine for happiness
To refine into mindfulness
So many blessings and such tenderness
All dependent on my determination

                         To love my life

When the drum beat is felt
              And the breath is robust
It's simple to love any given moment
To trust it's right and good for me to own it

Can I so simply own my sadness?
           Sit in its sharpness?
Hear its storytelling without prejudice?
              Not feel it monotonous?

Can I view it without subscribing
To an aesthetic which views a wilted flower
As less than a full bloom?

    If I can also love life for pricking
           There's no need to get beat down

To love all emotions for the lessons they
bring
Is how I'm learning to love my life.

Life thus loved with loyalty,
Brings opportunity
Daily, to suck the sweet
Nectar from the flower

To kiss the joys and pains as they fly

All things felt
And held in proportion

Yes!
I love my life

I love the choices I've made

I love the power to move
To a new equilibrium
Wild and unlasting as time
shall prove

I love the chance to win and lose

This masterpiece of life
Defies simple description
Despite all my sallies to make sense of it

My life remains
A mystery to me

SMOOTHING

As days go by
Her absence sustained
The pain is drained
Out through the tear ducts

I'm heartened vastly
By all of my allies
Animal, vegetable, mineral
Who meet me disheveled

Who listen to the poetry
As it looks for its level
And hold a mirror with
Their own tales of mettle

They carve out, with their patient
Compassion, a shelter
Blessing this mess
And I'm held there, intact

A passing protection
As the pain is unpacked
That demanding task.
Baby, witness me grow!

Together we are sanding
The rough surface of sadness
And with every pass of the paper
A little bit smoother

A little bit easier
With every storytelling
The compelling commonality
Our too human tragedy

A tapestry of our common feeling
Is being weaved
As we walk along this
Road of recovery

NUMB

Numbness is the mask I wear
When it smolders
When it costs too much to love

When I can't bear to ask
What even is this for?
Why am I alive?

When I remove myself
From where I used to thrive
Ye, become unglued

I grasp the mask
Is that what I should do?
Or else a mirror seek

To search my soul
And take myself to task
Or somewhere in between

The river runs below
Underneath the mask
That's soothing to the ear

A far-off sound
Not ready to be near
Not ready to be found

And all the soothing sounds
Of wind and leaves and birds
And insects abound

They decorate my mask
I sit unperturbed
A numbness quite profound

Shrouded in this cloak
Inside the heart of stone
Sweet asylum bespoke

Then I spoke aloud
"I'm no longer in pain"
So I guess there's hope?

When it costs too much too love
Camouflage is green
The mask is just a screen

With a thousand holes
A porous dream
Too poor to love

Too ashamed to scream
The mask comes from above
Cold comfort to mete

But it's just a mask
Can it hope to change
Whatever lies beneath?

Numbness that steadies
A plaster cast, agreeable yoke
Karma yoga for broken folks

When the mess is vast
Numbness is the mask
That suits the scope

THE GIFTS

In the brief time of our
Togetherness

I was so abundantly blessed
When I add it up

The gratitude heart
Overflows the cup

There was the gift of your excitement
Nervousness when we would talk
That made me feel immense
Because I was amusing you

There was the gift of your attention
When you read my second book
On the airplane, in one big bite
You carried me with you
In the desire to know me

There was the gift of sculpture
Picked off a gallery wall
That recalled to us my father
You sent me outside to buy it on the sly

Silly woman, darling flower
There was the gift of your body
A sharing so complete
We breathed the life of one another
Our chests and breaths entwined
And that remains

There was the gift of your desire
That clung to me with such eagerness
Insatiable, and I tasted you
As we were drowned in pleasure
Beyond measure, unforgettable

There was the gift of care
That I thought would last forever
And it was
It assuredly did

The gift of your struggle
The things you tried to reconcile
The vision lay in waiting
All the while

There was the gift of your blow off
That was so painfully sudden
Annihilating

Forcing me to begin again
The things you cleared out of me
There was the gift of armor
My tender heart
Too much exposed
You clothed me
With compassion and humility
The knowledge that God loves,
God loves us through our frailty

There was the gift of slowness
Which you wanted to show me
And finally did sow in me
Alertness. Appreciation
And the greatest
Of slownesses
Finality

There remain some gifts still in the mail
I'm certain to receive some day
Seeds planted by the great gardener
To sprout in their season
Perennial
Gratitude

ADAPTATIONS

As days
   Go by

My nervous system
Isn't synced with hers anymore

We no longer co-regulate

I knew
      This would happen
                     Inevitably
And I accept that.
                     Equivocally

I still have
Moments
But I have changed.

                  I dreaded this change.

Even the grieving
Is mostly done.
Not even that
Have I to cling to.

This whole precious episode,
The love
      The need
            The hurt

Shrinking, all shrinking
Into the past tense.

Inexorably
Becoming an artifact of my history

Like a tattoo, some amusing memories

Bludgeoned on
My permission foregone
Or never any matter

Ultimately even the suffering
Has been a tie to her.
Now the bond is fading.

      Cascading

        Time
        Moving
          Me on.

COMPASS

So we are
Separated,
We are so
Scattered

But it's just as she ordered

Whatever

Curtains of fog
Hang opaquely around you
I do not get to see

Whatever

Emissions come through
Seem to be carefully considered
Visions of what you should do

We

Remain in relationship
However tenuous.

You are magnetic north

No matter how far I travel
We remain linked
Even as it all unravels

No one knows for how long.

You are like so many songs
Stuck inside my head.
Are the lyrics a direct

Transmission from heaven?

ELECTRIC

Falling in love with you
Was so electric
It happened so fast
That wasn't I expected
My memories shifted
After being rejected
But falling in love with you
Was so electric

MORBID DOUBTS

Was it inevitable
That she would abandon me
Before she could be abandoned?

Ouch!
Myshkin!
Why must I think such thoughts?

I don't know.
I'm a scorned man
In a fictitious scenario.

The woman that I thought I knew
And her motivations
Tuned into like radio stations.

Hurt feelings crystalized
As strange religious artifacts
To maintain the force of a fiction
Yet undefined.

But who is the ghost writer
Of these peculiar characters?

Is she damaged goods?
Too easily manipulated?
Or is that a mirror I see?

I

    Am

        Weeping

For the imperfections
    We are heir to

Ashamed of theses doubts and denigrations
Arising only from a place of weakness

        I yearn
            To make choices
        That HONOR my soul

It's too big to fit into one view.
The perspectives that we do choose,
Actively loosen screws
So that we contribute to the active truth
By the choosing.

So what to do?

MIRROR BABY

In this bizarre transition,
While you create space

It's become apparent
Counting mistakes

Just how many I make,
        And the cost of assumptions

Like in the way
That fear or hope will sway
Us when we
Crave, or dread a spoken word
Attachment sucks the vitality of life
Like a blood leech
                Or an apple worm

When God acted in you to part us
With the vision
Why wasn't I there to dig into it?

My inner child clamored
                For attention

So I attended

Raw

I went to excavate,
To dwell among the bones of my brokenness
Searching for something I could contend
with.

God did not come to my tent in the night
He only gave me your word
But all I heard was

"You're not enough"

I am what I am
And it may not match what you need
But only notice
How ready I was to bleed
To needlessly assume and suffer
Assume, and get in my own way

Astoundingly I take away
From this blessed mess

    To ask clarifying questions.

    To rest.

    To go slow reacting.

Such somatic treasures
That I can hold in my heart
Through this untimely tearing apart

    "Sweet child of mine,
    Mirror baby.
    I'm going to hold you
    While we listen
    To the unfolding story.
    We won't believe the worst,
    From the first,
    Now will we?

    From now on
    We will wait to see more clearly"

KINTSUGI

Why would God create a flawed world?

Why should we suffer?

Why should we die?

Who can explain the use of a broken heart?

Why should we be tested only to fail?

Leather dragged across the sword

When you look in my eyes
You can see the lines of age

We smile at each other

And nod our heads

It is done

At the end of the day
The rabble crowd around the fire
To steal a little warmth

Is that why I love you so much?

When I look at you,
I see something surpassing perfection.

Everywhere you are bent,
I kiss

I see your faults,
Every crack

It's how the light gets in.

I want to know your brokenness by heart.

For you I have the resin

Your sharp edges

Our willingness

God holds
You in his artisan hands

Every fracture is

Filled with gold

CANCELED

You know that feeling
When you find a new series on Netflix
And it is absolutely the best thing ever
It has incredible, interesting characters
And a strong flow of action which seems to
be building
Towards something meaningful and
profound

And then...
    It gets canceled after the first season!

And I'm like WTF man!

How in God's name could you cancel
        This?
When all this is permitted?

It leaves me feeling so sorry
For all the episodes of our life
Scrapped on the cutting room floor
Despondent that the world will never
Get to see the shape of us as a unit
As we pass through the seasons

And that WE
Will never get to live them...

LIPS BRUISED

After all this time
Wondering what
Meeting again
Would be like

        We meet
        With bruised lips

Queen of cats
This table between us
Our hands entwined
Timing, proportion
The mathematics of distance
Decimated in an instant

The dissonance of our human noise
From the music of birdsong
You just want to walk along
The trails at the sanctuary

Your prayer is full of praise of nature
You're ready to go on without me.
Whatever that costs,
You're prepared to pay

Not a day goes by that I don't think of you
And…

Why can't I walk with you?

I think we both know.
But…

Our knowings go
Down separate paths
At that fork
In the yellow wood

Why can't I walk with you
With my eyes closed
My hand on your shoulder
Yours on the small of my back
I've shoes, strength and stamina
But there's something lacking…

> Kindly, lord
> Deliver it
> Some day

DREAMS

How I would love to sleep beside you,
      Once more
If only it could be arranged.

To twine with thine
For one last passage through the dark
To feel your warmth and register
Your preciousness in my arms

I imagine it would be
A pleasure over sweet to say
      "Goodnight my dear"
To feel you there,
Smell your hair.

Hold you, as night drifts by,
      Too quickly
            Into Day

Whatever joy that closeness sparks
Goes down
To be felt
In the sleeping heart
Warm coals
Not fire
Passion and love
Born of a grateful heart

The deepest and sweetest
For those coupled hours meet,
Hold you, feel you,
Grounded to the earth

Then in the land of dreams
I would somehow acquire
Whatever coins the ferryman may require
To take us forward double slow

Float

For as long as we could go,
Through all the episodes
Of our canceled love
Unbound by that fate

To reside again for awhile
In that harmony
Where the child in you
Played with the child in me.

To bask in the glow of your smile
In this innocent world
Be allowed to linger
Longer than the waking world
Ever delivered

Dazzled by the Seussian sculptures
We would remote create

As our subconscious' frolic and play
In that limitless limbic plain

All the hurt and loss and pain
Banished from the brain
For the span of twixt and twain

Together,
A closer walk with thee.
And then…

Awaken.

Could I calmly face the morning?
Surrender what was lost and found
Lost again

But…
Peace

Why speak of dreams,
And all things returning true
All simply because
I slept better beside you

REUNION

Seeing you tonight
It was done
Just like that
A snap of the fingers
Your hard hands
Across the maple table
The dim light
Veiled dining room

Your hands in my hands
My thumbs on your palms
The realness of you
Asserting itself again
In our hands touching

Meeting you in the driveway tonight
I took so much delight
In your knowing, grinning smile
As I pulled the car up on the lawn.

You love the kind of trouble I am.
Who can love me like that?
Did I notice you weren't trying?
What could be more charming?

Then we circled up to drink cacao
I sat there beside you like a puppet, taut.
Trying to feel you without looking.
I only wanted to look

                        And look,

You told me

                "Stop looking at me"

But I could feel your attention.

What on earth are we going to do?

Place your bets
The field is open
It doesn't much matter what we do

We've done and undone it all by now

RESILIENCE

Lover, I noticed you sweating
About some mistakes along the way
Wringing your hands in silence
Only willing to whisper
        "You were innocent, I took that away"

Baby you didn't break me,
I've got a back much stronger than that!
  You didn't wreck me,
                You just tousled my hair.
Maybe you drove me to drink for a while...
Do I have a hangover?
                I don't care.
I had a helluva good time!

Baby, you worry that you crushed me?
Do I look crushed?
                Don't answer that
                Sarcastic actress
                I feel fantastic

You might have rugged my trust...
But what does that really mean to me?
Nothing ventured, nothing gained.
Winning and losing are sides of a coin
married
And I've got resilience like rain!

I bet you think you corrupted me honey?
Or caused me too much pain?

Too much pain?!

Pain's good!

I'll take pain any day.
Legitimate suffering has
The power to purify and make wise
  I'm alive,
    Engaged and
      Ready to play.

Beloved
  You were like a thunderstorm.

    You came intense,
    Lit up the whole night sky.
    Your patterns, electric
    Indelibly etched on my brain

I danced in your fury
And
I fell to the ground.
But…
Would you believe it, baby?

    Aykaymaway kleen
    I came away clean!

NAME

Just randomly woke in the night
Remembering that I love your name
It's something beyond the letters
And their ordering

It's something beyond the syllables
                                 and sound
My mouth makes when I speak it
Something more and less profound
Essentially, a feeling I get when I see it

As though I can see a portal into my future
Or a secret prayer for my soul
That nourishes and lifts me
A symbol for me to love and nurture

You move me in my life
I move around you
You are a great river stone
That my soul is ever flowing over

Every ripple of the river passing
With every drop of rain falling

I am reaching out to you
To meet me in the water
With loving heart forgiving

The prayer I'm unfolding
Is one for you
To give yourself to your life.

So I pronounce your name, Beloved
Summoning your purest form
Unscathed by the thousands of days
You've walked upon this earth.

Make your mistakes, Hallelujah!

Follow the Son,
Not by surrendering all to him
But using the gifts he gave you!

His harshest lessons
Were never meant to break your trust
But to awaken you.

You are the handler of all your limitations

I want to trust you
And I need you
To open to the idea
That you can trust me too

TO GRIEVE

Propped up on pillows
Gazing into my laptop

Tumbling down rabbit holes again...
Corrupt politicians and police.
Can't stop scrolling...

That's the least of my worries,
Planet's doomed to melt...

That wound is always felt
The soundtrack is always playing
Softly in the background

As I search for affordable housing
Polar bears drown

I try to be cheerful.
She doesn't help.

We seldom even meet.
For shame and estrangement.

I don't miss her all that much,
If it's just for me.
I live in

And swim through
    A culture
       That's forgotten how to grieve.

Grief is hidden seven layers deep
      Behind every reel and meme
        In the unnatural attention we
        Dump into the machine
         Grief in the time we keep

      Grief, a smell like cigarettes
      That lingers in clothing
        Imbued between we two
      I feel it and it overwrites me
          I get confused
What matters to me?

Before I die and take my leave…
Is there an elder,
Somewhere,
Who remembers how to grieve?

What good is my life?

   What can this little one do?

      And if I have to leave her forever

        Will I grieve that too?

TIME

In the time it takes
To exhale
A drawbridge can rise or fall

In the time it take for an arrow
To travel halfway
                              to your heart
Infinities lay in wait

In the time it takes for you
To hit me up
The moon can wane to new

The tides respond to the moon's pull
While we both do
What we have to do

Will we ever coincide again?

RECKONING

Angry at the inevitable
Every which way I go seems a blind alley
Maybe she's just not for me

I want to be strong for her
Maybe I'm not the one

But why does it feel as it does?
Why that pull?
What's actually blocking us?
Can I really believe there's nothing I can do?

If it's not something I'm failing at...
If she's not ready to meet me...

I wish I could do something about this.

She needs to take space.

If she needs someone to wait
To overtake fate
To manage while she gets ready
Someone to be steady
And only wait...

What kind of life is that for me?
With no promise and no guarantee
Only waiting with the hope that
Maybe one day she'll be
Good for me.

I'd rather just have some
Sweet reciprocity

ORAÇÃO ALLYSON

She was a radiant being
Bright as a sun
So full of compassion
Yellow flower fun

She so wanted
To be like our lord
That she always forgave
Every trespass

And the rough ones found
That here they could get away
With the rude games
They liked to play

Her boundaries bowed
And would never last
No matter how they hurt her
She knew God would always

Always rebuild her
Like a sand castle on the shore
With no walls to protect it
But God was all

The protection she needed
Then one morning she realized
That wasn't his plan
He wanted to expand
And establish more vastness
In her castle heart

God was so busy restoring
What they were busy destroying
The work couldn't proceed.
He needed HER to defend it

So he gave her the seeds
And the lessons to lead her
Watch her proceed to
Build boundaries for God.

GOODBYE

A connection that gathers
Holds close to the heart
A bundling together that
Becomes something more
For those who are enfolded
Into something larger than themselves
               A nation, a religion
               A team, a club
               A place to grow roots
               A family

          I love you too much
                To not
             Belong to you

I can't endure
Being torn from you
Whenever you get gone

          Together, but not good
          I'll take the other road

All that's essential bound inside my skin
All beyond the boundary
                         Goodbye

We've gone past the point of possible return
More than once

Now I don't believe I can trust you
Tomorrow I intend to say to you

                              Goodbye

And I feel like a student the night before a
Big exam
I am not ready
Maybe I didn't study

          I'm tired enough to sleep
          But I'm not shutting off the light

'Cuz just as soon as I sleep
Morning will creep up like a thief
Dawn a new day
That should promise me relief
When we say

                              Goodbye

But I'm not ready to walk to your house
To print out the last poem
At the Staples on the way
So I'll delay sleep a bit longer

To make peace with what I hope to say

But what can I say?

We are like two cans of paint,
                        Blue and red
Blended together and forever changed
        Purple together, we became

                        It happened in the night
                        And in our shared breath
Goodbyes
As much as we may try
Never will the paint
Get back in their cans again

Be that as it may
I must say

                        Goodbye

It's deformed how we've performed these
last acts

And it's so tactless for me to have said that,
But...

                You can't seem to meet me
                Where I want to meet
                And I'm not prepared to repeat

These disastrous passages

I love myself too much to take your shit

No matter how well intended it is when you
explain it
I can't find patience to muddle through
The mud with you,
You disappear

Because actions speak louder than words

Goodbye

A connection that gathers and enfolds
A love that holds,
That holds space for one another
Bundling together that endures
Through all the weather
That's all I ever wanted from you

But you don't understand this
You believe you're on your own.
You only learn your lesson the hard way
And so, it is

Goodbye

EPILOGUE
WATERMELON-KIWI

I no longer speak to her;
She has blocked me
On all channels
And I don't see her
      From any of the previous angles.

But

When I'm in the dodge caravan
      I puff on a vape pen

That she discarded when we were dating

Again

"It's burnt," she said, and
Tossed it to the floor

I puff

Not because I like the flavor.

      It's not that.

It's just the last remaining artifact
From when I was in her favor.
Just a slender form of contact
It's three steps forward and two steps
back

Yet, I don't throw it out
With everything else that's ash
And gone away

  "Only until this cigarette has ended
   A little moment at the end of the day"

Someday soon,
When I put it
To my lips
It won't have anything left to give
No matter how I pull
To taste it still.

                    It is what it is.

Only then,
One more small goodbye
Will I say,
And surrender it to a waste bin.

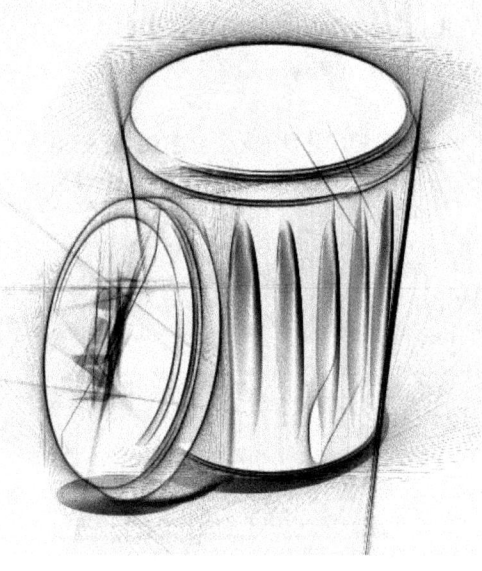

ARTISTS

DavidZydd

Sidharth Sharma

愚木混株 Cdd20

Nika_Akin

KaylinArt

MarkOblivious

Glenn J. Evans
(Cover Design)